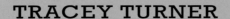

TRACEY TURNER

STAT ATTACK!

HORRID HUMANS

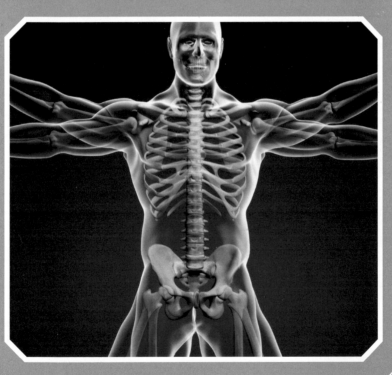

Franklin Watts
Published in Great Britain in 2017 by
The Watts Publishing Group

Credits
Series editor: Adrian Cole
Series designer: Matt Lilly
Art direction: Peter Scoulding
Photo acknowledgements:

Agency-Animal-Picture/Getty Images: 20cl. Gunnar Assms/Shutterstock: 21t.
Mikhail Blajenov/Shutterstock: 9cr. Bunyos/Dreamstime: 17br. Nigel Catlin/
FLPA Images: 7t. Hung Chung Chi/Shutterstock: 28br. claffra/Shutterstock:
8b. Cliparea/Custom Media/Shutterstock: 15tl, 15tc, 15tr, 15b, 23tl. Jemal
Countess/Getty Images: 29c. Creations/Shutterstock: 9tl. decade3D-anatomy
online/Shutterstock: 7cl, 17tr, 17bl. Jeanette Dietl/Shutterstock: front cover cl.
DM7/Shutterstock: 3r, 25, 26t, 26b. Mary Evans PL: 27cl. Gamma-Keystone/
Getty Images: 28l. Joe Goch/Shutterstock: 11t. gorilla images/Shutterstock:
9bl. Daniel Heuclin/Biophoto/FLPA: 21cl. Faisal Husain/Dreamstime: 2, 18t.
jareynolds/Shutterstock: 21cr. F. Jimenezmeca/Shutterstock: 13crb. Kaspri/
Shutterstock: 8tl. Vitaly Krivosheev/Shutterstock: 12tr. Ivan Kuzmin/Shutterstock:
6b. leungchopan/Shutterstock: 14bl. Liya Graphics/Shutterstock: 21cl.
mikevvzine/Shutterstock: 12br. Milkovasa/Dreamstime: 9tr. David Paul Morris/
The Brain Observatory Bloomberg/Getty Images: 18br. Piotr Naskrecki/Minden/
FLPA Images: 6c. Nerthuz/Shutterstock: 17cr. Orla/Shutterstock: 1, 16. Lefteris
Papaulakis/Shutterstock: 27t. Pascal Parrot/Corbis: 29t. Pathdoc/Shutterstock:
10c. Photoresearchers/FLPA Images: 21tl. Paul Popper/Getty Images: 18bl. Raj
Creationzs/Dreamstime: 9br. Robert Remen/istockphoto: front cover c. Roblan/
Shutterstock: 23tr. rook76 /Shutterstock: 27cr. Paul Schlemmer/Shutterstock:
3l, 19tl, 19tr, 19c, 19bl. Science Pictures Co/Alamy: 21tr. Russell Shively/
Shutterstock: 13tr. Thorsten Smidtt/Shutterstock: front cover cr. sunsetman/
Shutterstock: 24t. Kampol Taepanich/Shutterstock: 20br. tankist276/Shutterstock:
11b. Andrei Tarchyshnik/Shutterstock: 23cr. Michael Taylor/Shutterstock: 7cr.
Thedesignersdinner: 10t. TTStudio/Shutterstock: 13cl. Undrey/Shutterstock:
13cr. vistudio/Shutterstock: 17cl. Yury Vlasenko/Shutterstock: 12bl. Hong Vo/
Shutterstock: 13clb. Wikimedia Commons: 29b. John Wollworth/Shutterstock:
8tr. xpixel/Shutterstock: 13b. Yongchar-kittiyaporn/Shutterstock: 12tl. Zurijeta/
Shutterstock: 5. Zygotehasnobrain/Shutterstock: 21cr.

Dewey number 612
ISBN 978 1 4451 2753 8

Printed in China

Franklin Watts
An imprint of
Hachette Children's Group
Part of The Watts Publishing Group
Carmelite House
50 Victoria Embankment
London EC4Y 0DZ

An Hachette UK Company
www.hachette.co.uk

www.franklinwatts.co.uk

CONTENTS

Introduction

Did you just hear a sort of grunting kind of noise? That's because this book is absolutely bursting with information about the human body. In it you'll discover essential facts about deadly diseases, human parasites, bones, muscles and the human brain. Hide in a cupboard as you find out about the doctors who carried out human experiments, and gasp at the impressive body-bending tricks some people can do.

As well as facts and stats, there are quizzes to test your human body knowledge. In fact, let's have one now. Before you start reading the book, see if you can answer these questions:

1) What's your body's largest organ?

2) Which gas makes up most of a fart?

3) Where's the smallest bone in your body?

Read on to find out if you're right. →

Prepare to stuff your brain with hundreds of amazing facts and statistics until it's ready to explode!
The publishers would like to point out that they take **NO** responsibility **WHATSOEVER** for exploding brains.

Human Vital Statistics

To save you time measuring your small intestine or counting all the people on the planet, here are some quick statistics about horrid humans like you . . .

STAT ATTACK!

Number of human beings in the world: 7 billion (roughly)

Average height: 175 cm (adult men); 162 cm (adult women)

Number of bones in the human body: adults 206; newborn babies 270 (some bones fuse together)

Number of teeth: 32 adult teeth; 20 baby (milk) teeth

Largest organ in the human body: the skin, around 2 m squared (in an average adult)

Average length of small intestine: 6 m (in an adult)

Average weight of adult human brain: 1.3 kg

Eight Deadly Diseases

There's a terrifying number of nasty diseases that can kill you, and here is a small but grisly sample. Each one has a deadly rating, to show how likely the disease is to be fatal, and a revolting rating to show how horrible it is to be suffering from it. You definitely don't want to catch any of them! By the way, these diseases are all caused either by germs or tiny parasites, rather than other things going wrong with your body.

1 · BLACK FEVER

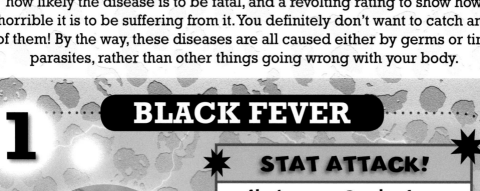

STAT ATTACK!

Also known as: Dumdum fever, kala azar, visceral leishmaniasis

Cause: tiny parasites transmitted by the bite of a sandfly

Symptoms: fever, weight loss, tiredness, swelling of liver and spleen

☠ **Deadly rating: 10/10** ☠

Revolting rating: 8/10

2 · RABIES

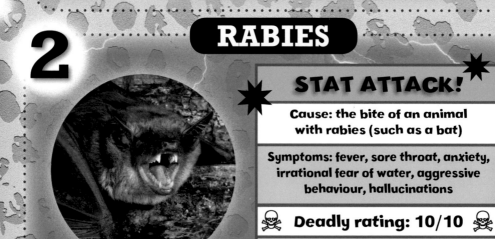

STAT ATTACK!

Cause: the bite of an animal with rabies (such as a bat)

Symptoms: fever, sore throat, anxiety, irrational fear of water, aggressive behaviour, hallucinations

☠ **Deadly rating: 10/10** ☠

Revolting rating: 10/10

3 SLEEPING SICKNESS

STAT ATTACK!

Also known as:
African trypanosomiasis

Cause: a tiny parasite transmitted by the bite of a tsetse fly

Symptoms: headache, pain, itchiness, swollen glands, anxiety, tiredness in the day but unable to sleep at night

 Deadly rating: 9.5/10

Revolting rating: 8/10

SMALLPOX

4

STAT ATTACK!

Cause: highly contagious virus

Symptoms: fever, headache, aches and pains, rash of pus-filled scab-covered blisters all over the body, open sores in nose and mouth

 **Deadly rating: 9/10** (but – good news! – the disease has been wiped out)

Revolting rating: 10/10

BUBONIC PLAGUE

5

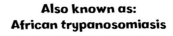

STAT ATTACK!

Also known as: the Black Death

Cause: bacteria transmitted by the bite of a flea

Symptoms: fever, aches and pains, huge, painful, egg-sized swellings in the groin, armpits and neck, known as 'buboes'

 **Deadly rating: 6.5/10**

Revolting rating: 10/10

EBOLA

6

STAT ATTACK!

Also known as: EVD
(Ebola Virus Disease)

Cause: a virus spread by the blood and other body fluids of an infected person or animal

Symptoms: headache, weakness, fever, diarrhoea and vomiting, rash, bleeding (inside the body as well as outside)

 Deadly rating: 5/10

Revolting rating: 9/10

CHOLERA

7

STAT ATTACK!

Cause: bacteria from an infected person's waste products transmitted in food or water

Symptoms: vomiting, watery diarrhoea, signs of dehydration including sunken eyes and wrinkled skin, bluish-grey skin

 Deadly rating: 5/10

Revolting rating: 9/10

MALARIA

8

STAT ATTACK!

Cause: tiny parasite transmitted by a mosquito bite

Symptoms: headaches, tiredness, fever, coughing, vomiting and (in severe cases) yellow skin, coma

 Deadly rating: 4/10

Revolting rating: 9/10

Dreadful Diseases Quiz

1 If you had bluish-grey skin, **which of these diseases might you have?**

a) Malaria   **b)** Cholera   **c)** Rabies

2 Which of these diseases is transmitted by a sandfly?

a) Black fever   **b)** Malaria

c) Bubonic plague

3 Which of these diseases is also known as the Black Death?

a) Ebola   **b)** Black fever   **c)** Bubonic plague

4 Which of these diseases might you catch if you are bitten by an infected animal?

a) Smallpox   **b)** Cholera   **c)** Rabies

5 Which of these diseases has been effectively wiped out?

a) Smallpox   **b)** Rabies   **c)** Ebola

6 How is malaria transmitted?

a) Mosquito poo   **b)** Mosquito bite

c) Flea bite

Dreadful answers **on page 30**

9

Seven Farting Facts

Yes, it was only a matter of time before we lowered the tone . . .

1 Farts are caused by taking in air as we eat and drink, and also by gas-making bacteria inside our gut.

2 Some foods make you more prone to farting than others: baked beans, cabbage, Brussels sprouts and fizzy drinks, for example. Chewing gum can make you fart more too because you swallow more air.

3 Some foods produce smellier farts than others. Meat and eggs are often smelly-fart culprits, but it varies from person to person.

4

In Cameroon, the Komas tribe hold a farting dance competition. People prepare themselves by eating lots of fart-producing foods for several days beforehand. The loudest, longest farts win!

5

Farts are mostly made up of odourless gases (see page 12). Only a small amount – less than 1 per cent – are smelly. Unfortunately it's sometimes very smelly indeed.

6

On average, adults fart about 14 times a day and produce roughly half a litre of gas.

7

In case you want to impress someone with your sophistication, the posh word for fart gas is...

'flatus'

FIVE FART GASES

1 CARBON DIOXIDE (CO2)

This gas makes up most of a fart, and it doesn't smell (CO_2 is also in the air you breathe out).

2 HYDROGEN (H)

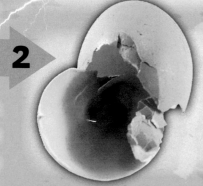

Hydrogen doesn't smell, but hydrogen sulphide, also found in farts, does. In fact, it smells very badly indeed (think rotten eggs).

3 METHANE (CH4)

This gas is produced by bacteria, and it's highly flammable. Not everyone has methane in their farts, though.

4 NITROGEN (N)

Nitrogen makes up most of the air we breathe and ends up in farts because we swallow air. It reacts with other chemicals to make two especially smelly compounds called indole and skatole.

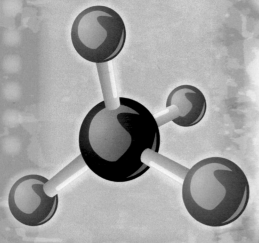

5 OXYGEN (O)

Oxygen is also present in farts from the air we breathe, but there's hardly any of it at all.

Ten Black Death Cures You Wouldn't Want to Try:
True or False?

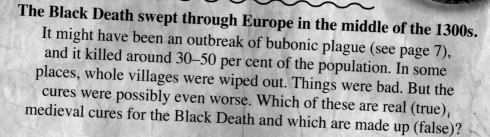

The Black Death swept through Europe in the middle of the 1300s. It might have been an outbreak of bubonic plague (see page 7), and it killed around 30–50 per cent of the population. In some places, whole villages were wiped out. Things were bad. But the cures were possibly even worse. Which of these are real (true), medieval cures for the Black Death and which are made up (false)?

1. Drink your own wee twice a day.

2. Cut open a vein to 'bleed' the disease from the body.

3. Strap a live chicken next to the plague sores to 'draw out' the infection.

4. Whip yourself (so that God might think you've been punished enough).

5. Drink a mixture of powdered roasted eggshells, crushed marigolds, beer and treacle.

6. Eat crushed emeralds.

7. Apply a mixture of human poo, flowers and onions to the plague sores.

8. Drink a potion laced with powdered unicorn horn.

9. Drink the poisons arsenic or mercury.

10. Attach blood-sucking leeches to your body.

True or False answers on page 30

Ten Medical Names for Body Bits

Impress your family and friends as you casually drop these medical terms into the conversation (you could suggest that your little brother gets off his nates and helps with the washing-up, for example).

1. Brow – Supraorbital ridge

2. Ears – Pinna

3. Nostrils – Nares

4. Jaw – Mandible

5. Chin – Mentum

6. Chest – Thorax

7. Rib cage – Cavea thoracis

8. Fingers (and toes) – Phalanges

9. Spine – Vertebral column

10. Buttocks – Nates

THE THREE LONGEST BONES IN THE HUMAN BODY

I Thighbone (femur)
STAT ATTACK!

Average length: about 50 cm

II Shinbone (tibia)
STAT ATTACK!

Average length: about 43 cm

III Lower leg bone (fibula)
STAT ATTACK!

Average length: about 40 cm

THE THREE SMALLEST BONES IN THE HUMAN BODY...

...ARE ALL FOUND INSIDE YOUR EAR.

These tiny bones vibrate when your eardrum is struck by a sound wave, and turn the vibrations into waves that travel through your inner ear. The three bones together are known as ossicles, and were given their individual names because they look a bit like a stirrup, anvil and hammer (their Latin names are in brackets).

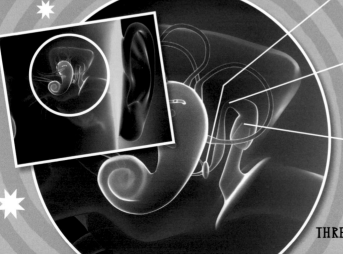

STAT ATTACK!

I Stirrup (stapes)
Average length: about 2.5 mm

II Anvil (incus)
Average length: about 5.5 mm

III Hammer (malleus)
Average length: about 8 mm

SKELETON QUIZ

USE THE INTERNET TO HELP RESEARCH THE ANSWERS TO THESE QUESTIONS.

Where on your body would you find a ball-and-socket **joint?**

a) Hip and shoulder   **b)** Wrist and ankle   **c)** Elbow and knee

1

2

If you fell on your coccyx, **which part of your body would hurt?**

a) Foot   **b)** Head   **c)** Bottom

3

Where would you find your sacrum?

a) Spine   **b)** Hand   **c)** Skull

4

What's your patella?

a) Kneecap   **b)** Wrist bone   **c)** Eye socket

5

6

What does your cranium **protect?**

a) Heart   **b)** Brain   **c)** Liver

What's the elbow bone **also known as?**

a) Humerus   **b)** Radius   **c)** Ulna

BONY ANSWERS ON PAGE 31.

Seven Brain-bending Facts

1 The human brain is the most complex organ of any living thing in the world, and on average weighs 1.3 kg.

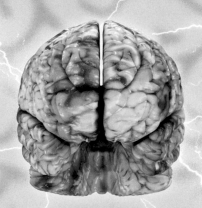

2 All your thoughts, feelings and actions are controlled by your brain, from feeling afraid to playing football to multiplying fractions. You have tens of thousands of thoughts every day.

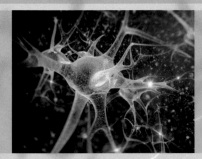

3 Neurons are cells inside the brain that transmit signals down pathways called synapses. There are about a 100,000,000,000 (one hundred billion) neurons in an average brain, and different types deal with different tasks in the human body.

4 Most of your brain's information is stored in the cerebral cortex, the surface of the brain, which allows us to sense things, think and remember. It's squished into wrinkles because it's tightly packed – you'd need a much bigger head if it wasn't.

5 There are several types of glial cell which help neurons. Some glia eat and digest dead brain cells.

6 Different parts of your brain are responsible for different things, and scientists are finding out more and more about which bit does what. There's an area of the brain that deals with recognising different faces, and a different one for remembering people's names.

7 The brain has three layers of protection: the scalp (the skin and hair on your head), the skull (cranium) and a membrane covering the brain and the spinal cord.

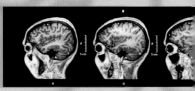

Two Famous People
Who Had Their Brains Removed

Don't worry – their brains were removed after they'd died . . .

✳ ALBERT EINSTEIN ✳

Albert Einstein was a brilliant physicist and general scientific wonder, and most people think of him as a genius because of the ground-breaking theories he came up with.

When Einstein died in 1955, Dr Thomas Harvey removed his brain and sliced it into pieces to try and work out if there was anything different about the great scientist's brain. Some differences from normal brains were found in Einstein's brain, including unusual grooves in the part of the brain that's used for mathematical reasoning.

✳ VLADIMIR LENIN ✳

Russian revolutionary **Vladimir Lenin** died in 1924. He was a radical political thinker, and such a hero to the revolutionaries that they decided to keep his body for as long as possible – it was embalmed and is still kept on display in his tomb in Moscow. His brain was also preserved, then cut up into more than 30,000 slices. It's kept in the Moscow Brain Institute.

FIVE IMPRESSIVE (BUT USELESS) BODY TRICKS

1 LICKING YOUR OWN ELBOW

Can you do it? Most people can't, but if you have a fairly short upper arm and a long tongue, and you're pretty flexible, you might be able to. You're having a go now, aren't you?

2 RAISING ONE EYEBROW

Few people can do this, but when they want to look sceptical, or like an evil genius, they can do it in style. You can teach yourself how to raise one eyebrow, but it'll take a long time and plenty of patience (stand in front of a mirror and raise your eyebrows while holding one of them down – eventually your brain will learn which muscles to control).

3 LICKING YOUR NOSE OR CHIN

Again, most people can't do this, but there are some people with especially long tongues who can.

4 WIGGLING YOUR EARS

This is a rare talent. Again, you can learn how to do it with hours of patience, determination and a mirror.

5 HAVE YOU EVER TRIED . . .

. . . raising your right foot and circling it clockwise while drawing the number six in the air with the index finger of your right hand? Why ever not? You probably couldn't resist trying this out immediately, so you might have already discovered that your foot seems to change direction of its own accord. It's like an extreme version of patting your head with one hand while rubbing your stomach with the other.

Six Uninvited Guests

Here's a thought: every square centimetre of your face is home to millions of bacteria.

It's all right – you don't need to go and have a bath or anything. Bacteria are our friends (at least, some of them are) and it's perfectly normal to be crawling with these single-celled organisms, as well as all sorts of other tiny living things. However, there are also some creatures that set up home on your body that you will definitely want to get rid of. Here are a few examples of some uninvited guests . . .

1 Demodex mites

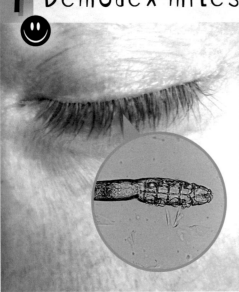

Mites are related to spiders, scorpions and ticks, and these tiny ones live in almost everyone's **eyelashes** (and on their faces). Yes, they're probably wiggling about on yours, right now. **They've been found living on humans all over the world.** They have eight short, stubby legs at the front end of their sausage-shaped body.

✷ STAT ATTACK!

Size: 0.3 mm	Special features: tiny claws and scales

2 Head lice

Maybe you've hosted **head lice** at some time in your life. These little insects live on your **scalp**, where they breed, lay eggs and die. They're most common in children's hair because children are more likely to put their heads close together – head lice crawl from one head to another, they can't jump or fly. They make most people's heads itch, and can cause a rash if you're allergic to their **poo**.

✷ STAT ATTACK!

Size: up to 3 mm	Special features: hook-like legs

3 Body lice

Body lice look exactly like head lice, but instead of laying their eggs in human hair, they do it in clothing. Body lice spend the rest of their time roaming about the body, drinking people's blood. Some body lice carry bacteria that can cause the **deadly disease typhus**.

✱ STAT ATTACK! ✱

Size: up to 3 mm	Special features: six hook-like legs

4 Scabies mites

These tiny **mites** are skin parasites that cause terrible itching in their human hosts. They eat their way into the skin and lay eggs, which then hatch out into more mites. They especially like warmer areas – **under arms**, for example.

STAT ATTACK! ✱

Size: up to 0.4 mm	Special features: suckers, claws and spines

5 Botfly larvae

WARNING: don't read this if you're squeamish.

The human **botfly** buzzes around Central and South America, every so often attaching its eggs to the underside of a mosquito. When the mosquito goes to bite someone, a botfly egg drops off and hatches, **burrowing under the skin**. The maggot grows fat on its host for up to three months. Then it wriggles out and turns into a botfly. You could seal up its air hole then remove the dead maggot with tweezers if you want it gone sooner!

STAT ATTACK!

Size: 2 cm or more!	Special features: long jaws and tiny spines

6 Bed bugs

Bed bugs don't live on your body, but they do like to come out at night to **drink your blood**. They're small, reddish-brown insects that hide during the day and come out when they detect body heat and CO_2.

STAT ATTACK!

Size: up to 4.5 mm

Special features: sawing mouthparts that inject anti-clotting and pain-killing chemicals

INTERNAL ⚙RGANS QUIZ

You probably don't give much thought to your insides – they just get on with stuff without you having to worry about it. Find out how much you know about the hard-working organs inside your body . . .

1 How often does your heart **beat** at rest?

a) About 40 times a minute

b) About 70 times a minute

c) About 120 times a minute

2 Which internal organ includes bronchioles?

a) Heart

b) Lungs

c) Gall bladder

3 Where is bile **made?**

a) Stomach

b) Bladder

c) Liver

4 Where do you find gastric juice?

a) Intestines

b) Pancreas

c) Stomach

5 How long is the average person's large intestine?

a) 7 m

b) 3 m

c) 1.5 m

6

How long is the average person's small intestine?

a) 6 m

b) 3 m

c) 1.5 m

7

The gall bladder and pancreas are part of which system?

a) Digestive

b) Reproductive

c) Respiratory

8

How many gallstones should you have?

a) 0   **b)** 2   **c)** 6

9

Which gas do you breathe out most from **your** lungs?

a) Oxygen

b) Nitrogen

c) Carbon dioxide

10

Where would you find your primary auditory cortex, Wernicke's area, **and** Broca's area?

a) Lungs

b) Brain

c) Intestines

Internal organ answers on page 31

Four Faecal Facts

Faeces, or poo, is a vital part of the human body's functioning. We eat food, take what we need from it, then what's left over comes out of the body in smelly lumps.

WE'RE SORRY, BUT THERE IT IS. Here are some facts about faeces:

1 Usually, poo is made up of about three quarters water and one quarter solid matter.

2 The solid content of poo includes dead bacteria (about 30 per cent), indigestible bits of vegetables (about 30 per cent), fats (10–20 per cent), other indigestible bits and pieces (10–20 per cent) and a small amount of dead human cells and protein.

3 People vary dramatically in the number, size and quality of the poos they produce every day. Some people might only do one every two days, some might poo several times a day, and all of them might still be healthy. How much food, and the type of food you eat are crucial factors.

4 The smelly chemicals in poo include indole, skatole and hydrogen sulphide (see page 12).

★ STAT ATTACK! ★

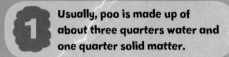

Average number of poos per day (adult): 1.5
Average weight of poos per day (adult): 175 g
Average percentage of solid matter: 25 per cent

Where Are You on the Chart of Poo?

If you go to see the doctor with some kind of poo-related problem, the chances are a special poo chart will be produced. Which type of poo do you do?

1 Small hard lumps. If your poo is like this, it might be painful, and shows that you're constipated.

2 A sausage made up of lumps. You're a bit constipated.

3  A sausage with a cracked surface. Congratulations! This is an ideal poo.

4 A smooth sausage. This poo is also ideal!

5  Soft lumps. This is a bit diarrhoea-like.

6  Mushy. You have diarrhoea.

7  Watery, without any solid pieces. Oh dear! You have severe diarrhoea.

Three Marvellous Muscles

You wouldn't be able to do much without muscles – they help you run, jump, smile and play computer games, all by pulling your bones into different positions.

Here are three of them:

1 Gluteus maximus

These are the biggest muscles in your body, and you have two of them . . . they're the muscles of your buttocks (or nates if you want to be posh, see page 14). As well as providing some comfortable padding when you sit down, these muscles help you stand, crouch, sit and do all sorts of other things.

2 Deltoid

These muscles are at the tops of your arms. They let you swing your arms and raise them up or sideways.

3 Quadriceps femoris

This is a group of four big muscles in your front thigh. These muscles straighten your knee when you're running or walking.

Five More Marvellous Muscles

4 Biceps

These muscles work in partnership with your triceps to make your elbows move. Biceps bend your elbows . . .

5 Triceps

. . . and triceps unbend your elbows.

6 Pectoralis

These are your chest muscles, often known as 'pecs'. These muscles pull your arms forwards and in towards your body.

7 Rectus Abdominis

This is the 'six-pack' muscle, or 'abs', that lets you bend your body.

Deeper inside your body, you also have muscles that protect and support your organs, as well as cardiac muscle that makes your heart beat, and smooth muscle in your digestive system.

8 Masseter

You have two masseter muscles. They are your main jaw muscles, on each side of your face, and they pull your jaws together. They're assisted by other muscles when you chew. The masseter muscles exert the most force of any muscle in the human body.

Three Disgusting Doctors

Scientists have done some horrible things in the name of human health. Here are some who went beyond the call of duty in a rather disgusting way . . .

1

HIPPOCRATES

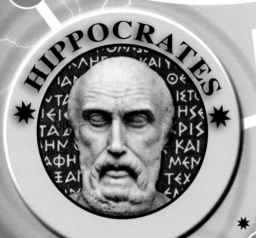

Known as the father of modern medicine, ancient Greek **Hippocrates** was one of the first doctors to observe diseases and keep records, and to realise that illnesses had a natural cause (rather than a supernatural one).

He was so committed to treating his patients that he sniffed and tasted their earwax, snot, urine and vomit.

2

BEAUMONT

3

SPALLANZANI

William Beaumont was a nineteenth century American army surgeon who carried out a series of truly disgusting experiments on a man who'd accidentally shot himself in the stomach, leaving a permanent hole.

Look away now if you've just had your lunch: Beaumont's experiments involved dangling different types of food into the man's stomach to see how long they took to digest.

In the eighteenth century, **Lazzaro Spallanzani** experimented with how food changed inside the body in an especially horrible way.

He ate food, vomited it back up, then ate the vomit. Then he ate the vomited vomit, and even the vomited vomited vomit. He was really sick.

Six Extreme Humans

The World's Tallest Person

STAT ATTACK!

Name: Robert Wadlow

Nationality: American

Lived: 1918-1940

Height: 272 cm (8 feet 11 inches)

2 The World's Tallest Woman

STAT ATTACK!

Name: Zeng Jinlian

Nationality: Chinese

Lived: 1964-1982

Height: 248 cm (8 feet 1.75 inches)

3 The World's Shortest Person

STAT ATTACK!

Name: Chandra Bahadur Dangi

Nationality: Nepalese

Born: 1939

Height: 54.6 cm (21.5 inches)

4 The World's Oldest Person

STAT ATTACK!

Name: Jeanne Calment

Nationality: French

Lived: 1875-1997

Age: 122 years 164 days

5 The World's Longest Fingernails

STAT ATTACK!

Name: Lee Redmond

Nationality: American

Born: 1941 (she started to grow the nails in 1979 and lost them in a car accident in 2009)

Length of each fingernail added together: 8.65 metres

6 The World's Most Tattooed Person

STAT ATTACK!

Name: Lucky Diamond Rich

Nationality: New Zealand

Born: 1971

Tattoos cover: 100 per cent of body, plus insides of eyelids!

Dreadful Diseases Quiz (page 9)

1b) The blueish-grey skin caused by cholera is a result of low oxygen levels in the infected person's blood. Cholera can be prevented by simply having access to clean water and good hygiene.

2a) Simple bed nets (like mosquito nets) can reduce transmission of Black Fever, along with using insect repellent and covering up skin.

 **3c)**

4c) Rabies can be transmitted by a number of animals infected with the disease, including: raccoons, foxes, bats, skunks and dogs.

5a) The last known natural case of smallpox occurred in 1977, and it was declared eradicated (wiped out) in 1980.

6b)

TEN BLACK DEATH CURES You Wouldn't Want to Try: True or False? (page 13)

Actually we didn't make any of them up! You'd have to be pretty rich to try some of them – the crushed emeralds, for example. The tusks of narwhals, a type of whale, were sold as unicorn's horns for ten times their weight in gold. The chickens, roasted eggshells and marigolds were cheaper options.

Skeleton Quiz (PAGE 16)

1a) The ball-and-socket joint in the hip and shoulder allows the greatest range of movement of any joint. The wrist and ankle are gliding joints, while the elbow and knee are hinge joints.

2c) Your bottom! The coccyx is often called the tailbone, and it's the last section of the spine, attached to the sacrum (see number 3).

3a) The sacrum is the triangular bone at the base of the spine.

4a   **5b**

6c) The ulna is one of the two bones in your forearm (the other one's the radius), and it ends in your elbow. The humerus is the bone in the upper arm – and, incidentally, it might be why people talk about the 'funny bone' (which is actually a nerve behind your elbow), because 'humerus' sounds just like 'humorous' (but isn't very funny at all, especially if you've just bumped it).

INTERNAL ⚙RGANS QUIZ (PAGES 22-23)

1b) Your heart beats about 70 times a minute at rest, but speeds up when you're doing something energetic like playing tennis.

2b) Your lungs contain air passages called bronchioles.

3c) In your liver. It processes the nutrients you've absorbed from food, and makes bile, a greenish-yellow fluid that helps digest fats.

4c) In your stomach. Gastric juice contains powerful acid that turns food into a smooth liquid. It's strong enough to strip paint!

5c) It's called the large intestine because it's much wider than the small intestine.

6a) The small intestine should really be called the long intestine. There's loads of it!

7a) They produce chemicals that help to break down the food we eat.

8a) None at all. Gallstones can form in your gall bladder, but they shouldn't be there. Sometimes they do no harm, but they can cause painful problems.

9c) You breathe out waste carbon dioxide. You breathe in oxygen from the air and your lungs transfer it into your blood.

10b) The primary auditory cortex detects sound, Wernicke's area helps interpret language, and Broca's area produces speech.

GLOSSARY

bacteria – A microscopic, single-celled life form that can cause disease.

coma – A deep sleep that can last for days or weeks, often caused by an injury.

compounds – A mixture of two or more things.

constipated – To have difficulty doing a poo.

contagious – When a disease can be easily spread from one living thing to another.

cranium – The part of the skull that encloses the brain.

dehydration – The loss of a large amount of water from the body.

diarrhoea – A condition where a person must go to the toilet often and their poo is very runny.

digest – To break down food into nutrients that can be used by the body.

embalmed – When a body has been preserved from decay.

glia – The connective tissue in the nervous system.

hallucinations – Things that are not really there – tricks of the imagination.

hosts – A living thing in which a parasite lives.

membrane – A cover or lining.

neuron – A nerve cell.

nutrients – A substance that provides everything needed for life and growth.

parasites – A living thing that lives in or on another living thing.

vibrations – Movement created in a gas, liquid or solid.

virus – A living thing that can only grow and multiply when it links to a living cell, often causing disease and infection to that cell.

INDEX